The Top Mistakes You Make Being Human

By

Benny Ferguson Jr.

The Top Mistakes You Make Being Human
By Benny Ferguson © 2014

ISBN:
978-1-7354117-5-0

Published by:
The Ferguson Company

Editor & cover design:
http://roxanec.wix.com/time-to-read.com

Welcome

What does it mean to be human? How does viewing yourself as a human being having an experience, change your experience? To the follower of the mass culture, it is not to shift the plane of thinking, but if you are the challenger of norms, you will quickly awaken to the knowing that spirit is from whence you came and spirit is where you will return. Understand the rules to the game and then you have the greatest opportunity to win.

Believing The Experiences Of Others Automatically Become Your Experiences

True, to each his own is the automatic balance between nature and mind. There is no maker of the seed of experience beyond you, the individual. Yes, your soul has a path of succession, growth, and expansion that is ideal for this physical experience, but it is up to you to follow the highest experience on your path toward its realization.

The cause of your journey, your experience lies within you. No matter what dire straits you are born into, the mind of the individual human being has massive power to pull and change environments to what they choose to prescribe. It is no secret that the mass mind has no bounds. It seeps into each home and curses the archetype with negative thoughts. Thoughts that damn the individual with experiences which they would never choose to have on their own.

Why would you let such a thing happen? The experience of one does not equal the experience of another. The wealthy of your lands live a completely different life and you accept that as true. Those who experience significantly less wealth and abundance, experience a different life and they accept that as true. However, when it comes to the actual selection of experiences, it becomes a task and a chore of disbelief. All the while the negative, low energy vibration existences of the world are impressed upon you, and you accept them as the only reality, when so many other realities of choice exist all around you.

What do you choose to create in the world for yourself? Look deep into your being and see what your soul desires. Is it to look upon breathtaking views? Is it to be in the company of other successful people? Is it to sail the seas alone? Is it to break a record? Is it to compete at the highest level in an event?

These are the questions only you can ask, and that only you can answer.

Each individual's experience is a choice. The seeds are sewn subconsciously, and no individual's experience is the same, even though they may appear to be similar.

Key:

Live your life with blinders on, blinders of the subconscious mind, blinders of the heart, and blinders of the soul. View the outside world with wonder and awe. Notice its majesty, its perfection, look to the light in every situation every interaction, but do not internalize experience. Look to your own heart, your own soul for your highest calling, for your highest choice of experience, and build it in your mind with focused thought and emotion. Live it often as it is true reality, and you will realize it in your physical experience.

Allowing Someone Else's Truth To Be Your Truth

That which is thought to be truth, other than the law abiding activity that governs the creation of your life and your experiences, is all up to question. It is subjective, and the result of one human being looking through the lines of their life and imposing that view on another.

Truth is a decision, and the deepest truth is to live in the presence of either the negative or positive energy that pervades the world…. It guides your thoughts. It is the undercurrent of your consistent feeling and emotions. It guides your habits of behavior.

The energy that you choose to allow to pervade your being the most consistently creates the flavor of your life.

Truth, truth is in the eye of the beholder. The activities of the world are governed by law. It is your choice to place your life in flow with the law or place your life at odds with it.

Uniquely, your life takes on its own meaning. Strategically, it will take on its own color. But if you allow it to be guided by the mind and activity of the masses, it will be dull, dreadful and frustrating, and early you will appear distraught and beaten.

Allow the masses to set their truth. Let them follow one after another in the blinding realm of experience, chasing the next shiny object, the next big thing.

They have been blinded by the lives that they do not want to live, and simultaneously set their focus, their inner power on the very things they do not want. They are creating the experience.

Why wander around in a life that is not of your creation? Why wander around in a life that isn't remotely what you would choose as an experience?

Key:

Set your inner sights on the life you want. Use your imagination to outline all interactions and all results. Summon the energy and emotion that you would feel upon completion, or acceptance, and allow the image and corresponding vibration to pull you toward it, attracting the resources, the learning, and the growth necessary to make the experiences you desire a permanent part of your life.

Following A Path Not Your Own

The path, metaphorically speaking, is the way by which you go about experiencing life. It consists of your job, your travels, your successes, your failures, and noting the theme that appears when you look back. It is noticing any patterns when you take a look or feel into what you have created in the world.

Are you participating in creating someone else's dream or are you actively creating yours?

To follow someone else's dream is to be influenced heavily by friends and family as to what you should do in life and what direction you should take. To follow someone else's dream is to have a desired experience, but to be so heavily influenced by the ideas of others that you neglect to even try. Or, your attempt is just a poor excuse for an effort at the life that you want.

To follow your path is being aware of the music that plays on the inside of you, and allowing that song to sing everywhere you go. It can be heard in the clothes you wear, the car you drive, the places you go, the people you associate with. If you follow your inner self, without hesitation you will realize the journey that is yours and yours alone. If you follow without fear, you will realize the experiences that are solely meant for you, and you will enjoy fulfillment.

Key:

The absence of fear is necessary when following, creating your own path in the world, for there is no road map or prior guide. There are individuals and wisdom to assist with the growth of you, but there is no one to tell you what is right or not right for you. There is no one to tell you what you should or should not be attempting or trying to do. No one knows your heart, or what your soul has in store for you.

Believing Your Connection To Source Goes Through Another Human Being

Your connection to Source is alive and well. It is not surprising that you seek this area of your life or feel drawn to some study of the unknown. Human beings have had some form of spiritual activity from the beginning. From the tribes of Africa to the Native Americans, there were spiritual practices and beliefs, ideas of a greater unity, a greater connection between all living things and something else, a giver of life, a giver of order, and a holder of universal perfection.

A macro outlook is that all things are created with a certain unison in mind, a balancing that occurs to ensure life for all, and this creation, this life is governed by law established by an essence, an intelligence that has been given many names down through the centuries, and carries many names now depending on the part of the world in which you live.

No matter what you call it, it is all the same. The only thing that matters is whether you are connected to it or not. Are you guided by that intelligence in your personal life? Do you allow it to be your ultimate answer or go-to in the good and the bad?

All things are a part of the whole. All things are permeated by that which brings life and the existence of the physical world in which you play and exist for a moment.

To whom do you belong?

If you ascribe to a particular organization that claims a name and route to Source, with rules that guide you along the way, be weary.

In fact, to connect with your Source requires nothing more than for you to be still and quiet in your mind. This has been the practice of all great spiritual teachers who have walked your planet, and it is all that is required for you to connect as well. When you look to the major spiritual traditions of your time, you will see various practices, all steeped in achieving the same goal, a personal connection with Source.

If you are not participating in the practice of stillness and mental clearing for greater connection to Source, you may be wasting your time, or participating in one of the many systems of control that have been set up by human beings with the basic, unconscious human calling at its core.

Key:

Your life force exists now as a part of Source. Inseparable, you are it and it is you. To allow this essence of life to fully flow through you, creating a world of wonder, as it was first intended, you must remove all ideas in mind that separate you from the possibility of health, relationship, wealth, abundance, and all other desires that are uniquely yours.

In the privacy of your own heart do you make this connection? You do not have to travel for miles, nor do you have to submit to another human being for divine guidance. You are the divine, and the necessary guidance is within. If you do feel the need to look outside yourself in the beginning, look for the practices that suit and feel correct for you in the moment.

Seeing Failure As An End

The experience of failure and even the thought of failure have been the bane of many would be successes. Your culture has created a sense of fear and embarrassment around the very nature, a basic human nature, to explore, try, venture into the unknown to the point that people hesitate and quit before they even begin. The very drive that built countries, that drove the exploration and development of new lands has been lost at the individual level.

Making mistakes and failing is not to be looked down upon. It is to be commended. It is to be favored, for this is the crux of learning. It is the crux of growth and expansion. The constant venturing out of children is what catapults their growth at light speed. It is what excites the spirit and tickles the mind. But at a point it becomes a negative, an unwanted, frowned upon trait to fail and make mistakes. Society, family, and friends prefer that you settle down and follow the normal path, adhere to the norms of society, and if you do not you are laughed at and frowned upon when you fall rather than cheered for your effort.

It is time to stand firm in your being human. Failure is not an end. In your history of inventors and challengers of social norms, it has never been an end; it has always resulted in a new beginning in understanding, belief, and possibility.

Only in failed attempts are the new roads and new opportunities discovered. Only in failed attempts is it known what will not work. Only in failed attempts are the depths of human potential revealed.

Key:

Fail!! Embrace mistakes!!! Couple your efforts with good judgment, firm data, and strong mentors as much as possible, but do not let the absence of the latter two stifle your drive, your burn to take action. Flush social norms. Stomp the way things have always been done under your feet and seek higher, newer, better ways to do things. Seek problems to solve in the world. Seek to break records or simply try something new. Your soul longs for growth and understanding, higher levels of experience. Do not let life as it stands or people as they stand stop your evolution.

Seeing Life As A Static Point Without Continuation

Life as a whole is not without its ups and downs. The natural scheme of things is to embody the pain or the bad, and to merely see the good as a blip in the exchange of thoughts and ideas that are present in the world to which you have turned your attention, but it is not permanent reality – physical experience – until you begin to focus on a single concept of experience.

Thy notice the good for the moment, but life, is a continuation and not a static point.

When you focus on any one happening in experience you freeze yourself in that moment and continue to relive that moment over and over again until you release it into the ether of ever moving consciousness.

If life is a continuation, what do you want to experience next, next, next? These are the only questions to answer. These are the images you focus on and make a permanent part of your mental playground.

The discussion of life and its particular workings is a conversation for the wise and still at heart, but to believe that the static nature of one individual's existence is the permanent life of another is a false premise. In the adults years of most individuals you find a hardening of the mind, a hardening of spirit, and a stiffening of what was once flexible, elastic expectation. Now, as children with grand expectations and desires become adults they buy into the reality that there is no escape from the norms of life that they see around them. There is no escape from the reality that appears real. There are no avenues to the life that is merely a figment of one's imagination. They neglect to see that their entire life to this point has been a continuing movement of their imagination from thought to experience.

What do you remember as desire manifest, from school, to college, to travel, to vacations, to the restaurant you went to? They all are materializations of thought. You have a choice as to whether you will continually create new thoughts, new experiences in your mind, or you will succumb to the static, repetitive thinking, believing in the norms of society.

Life only becomes a constant swirl of sameness when you allow your thinking to become centered on the same concepts, the same lifestyle, the same type of experiences.

Key:

Remember that you are a creator. Remember that multiple life experiences are being created all around you and the type of experience that calls to you is the one that you should focus on and give all of your mental effort and attention. There is no prize for buying into and believing in the pain and sadness that exists around you. However, there is wealth in your ability to create any life that you choose, moving your station to any position in the free world which your heart seeks to attain.

Seeing Relationship As Anything Other Than A Reflection Of Those Things That Need Clearing To Enhance & Further Your Connection To Source

Relationships are such a challenging undertaking in your time because so few fail to realize their reflective nature. All relationships that you create, come in contact or interact with are all a representation of some inner ideas or belief that you carry.

Some are beautiful, some are painful. Some are constant bothers yielding frustration, stress, and strain around every corner. Either way, they are reflections of you on some level or another.

The things that make you so angry, on the one hand, and the things that make you excited, on the other, are all parts of your inner makeup. The issues of life that create reaction within you are your own, and few experience life inwardly the same way you do, as consistently as you do.

So, to view the relationships in your life as anything other than the reflections that they are is to miss the learning that is present for you. It is to miss the growth and development that awaits and calls you from your soul.

Yes, the evidence of massive impact that relationship can have on you is all around. Setting your sights on the good qualities of an individual will shine a different light on their flaws and their mistakes. Setting your sights on the strengths of an individual rather than their weaknesses gives you grave insight as to the reasons behind their behaviors or into their motivations, and knowing these things make you stronger.

To the extent that you begin to let go of the nuances that make your blood boil, you will begin to see a different world in front of you. You may begin to notice that God is in all things. You may begin to notice that the sun rises and casts light even when you cannot see it. You may begin to notice that the instances you once thought worthy of your fire are not as serious as you thought. Taking opinions personally is not worth it anymore. Feeling disrespected is not worth it anymore. Taking misunderstandings to heart are counterproductive and take you even further away from the outcome that you truly desire.

The truth is that Source is the ultimate goal. Allowing Source to move through you awakens and creates a powerful pull of attraction to your goals. All seeds of frustration, anger, fear, and stress act to separate you from your Source. All ideas, together with triggering outside experiences, create a negative vibration within your mind and body that move you further away from power and unity with Source energy.

Love is a connector. Thanks and gratitude are connectors, and the more you venture to see and present these attributes in the world, in and through your relationships, the more in unison with Source you will be.

Key:

Recognize that the highs and lows of relationships are cues to your connection or lack of connection to your Source. The minute you begin to free yourself from the binds of ideas that cause frustration and stress, you begin to see life in a new light. The relationships that you desire, closely resembling the connection you permanently have with Source, are just outside of the ideas that keep you frustrated and stressed. And finally the joy you see and allow into your experience through relationships will be the joy from Source streaming into your life, for all is it and it is you.

Neglecting The Inherent Unity In All things And Their Operation Together

One of the biggest mass confusion mistakes the human being makes is believing in the illusion that all things are separate. When in truth all things at the core are connected, are one with the eternal Source.

The appearance of separation allows for the beauty of individual experience in the physical realm. The separation that appears to be enables each individual to know themselves as separate from one another. It is the perfect platform for experience and expansion.

It becomes a negative process only when the individual human being begins to believe in and function within the negative energies that pervade the outer crust of this dimension. Each individual has a choice as to which energy will sustain and embellish their life. The higher level energies and vibrations yield a life of unity and harmony. This life is filled with its obstacles and challenges, but they are experienced along a path of growth to fully experience and expand the individual's soul purpose. The lower level energies and vibrations yield a life of pain and constant suffering and frustration. This path is also filled with its challenges and obstacles, but they're repetitive due to the fact that the individual remains focused on the pain and strife of the world, focused on the negative aspects of experience, and therefore missing out on potential learning that develop one's inner most nature, being, and abilities.

The unity that pervades and connects all things is what enables the law of attraction to work in the life of the individual human being. A focus that is set on a particular goal or experience at once goes to work, drawing the resources, people, and information necessary for materialization. All exist now. Nothing is made or destroyed in energy. All exist and is merely repositioned, reapplied in different forms. A focused mind commands the flow of energy.

A focused mind moves through the inherent unity and connectedness of all things and brings together the resources, situations, and circumstances necessary for materialization. There is no need to concern yourself with whether your desire will affect the materialization of another's desire, because it does not. All works in unison with an infinite supply, provided for your use in the fulfillment of your soul's purpose.

Unity yes. Separation no. This is also why you continue to see and meet yourself, your inner most beliefs in others, in the people you meet. But you do not want to hear that. The person you are is the people you meet. That is why it is so imperative to mold yourself into the person and the experiences you wish to see in the world. There is no other way to influence and affect the change.

Key:

Know that all things are connected. Simply believe it intellectually until you realize and know it physically and experientially.

Begin the play and practice of curbing the cause of your experiences and your connection to the negative, low energies and vibration of the outer, physical realm. Begin the play and practice of curbing your subconscious beliefs/dominant ideas.

Seeking The Complications Of Life Rather Than Seeking Simplicity

The gifts that you wield in the world are your ticket to the abundant life. All who have realized their calling, or, in better terms, followed the track guided by their soul have realized the life meant for them.

Your gifts, however, if you have not discovered them, are covered, cloudy by a sea of complications and distractions. The remedy is to place a halt on your life and look inwardly for those activities, those experiences that you desire most, and then devise a plan to move in that direction whole heartedly with the absence of fear.

The stars of business, entertainment, and sports are not ones who have succeeded due to luck or precise calculation. This mistake is made because you cannot see the heart of a man or woman. Their immense success in an area of life is due to incredible focus and an indomitable will in which fear could find no home. They would not be distracted from their ultimate goal. This state of mind was the result of their following and knowing they were in use of their gifts to the world.

You also have gifts to the world, and there is a practice that would yield you all that you desire whether that is everything or nothing. But you must uncover your gifts, hone them, put them to use, follow the direction and guidance from your heart, and trust that all will work out in the end. You do not need to know all of the steps required, you merely must be in motion.

Simplicity will allow the blossoming of your gifts. Reduce the work load of your mind so that your natural tendencies and inclinations may come forth.

Reduce the focus of your projects from many to a few. Scattered mental energy weakens you. The more focus you can apply to a cause the stronger your effort and attraction will be.

Simplify your life with processes and systems that allow for seamless operation, allowing you to focus on more of the things that bring you joy and fulfillment. What you will find is that your gifts will be intimately tied to that which brings you joy, and that which brings you joy is also tied to riches and well-being.

Key:

Recognize those things which bring you joy. Place them all in a circle and notice the personal strengths, characteristics, and or attributes that rise to the surface. Encourage your subconscious being to reveal your gifts to you so that you can quickly get on the path to their utilization. Know that there is power in simplicity. Many and more create confusion and distraction. A few select choices that are all in line with your highest desires allow for a quick and steady flow of your power without the diffusion of energy due to an excess of choices and options.

Yes, chaos and frustration often precede great learning and understanding, but in daily operations, chaos of environment and mind equal weakness.

Nature Of Unconditional Love – The Right To Live

The true nature of Unconditional Love is light years away from what the mass of human beings claim is love.

Love as you would like to believe is actually a cry to fill the pieces of your heart, a heart that has been placed in shambles by other broken hearts that attempted to raise you from a young human being to an adult. Fear, neglect, inadequacy, loss, anger; all were the guides of those who attempted to love you and show you love. So, it is no surprise that you do the same.

Love does not have to be reciprocated for you to love. Love does not even have to be accepted for you to love. The Love you receive from Source just is, there are no restrictions or special qualifications.

As a human being in the physical reality, you have been taught the significance of right and wrong, and it has been described under the pretense that if another is not behaving or believing in accordance to what you believe is right then they are not worthy of your love. Again, Love just is. There are no special requirements.

From religious affiliation to sexual orientation, Love just is. To judge or cast blame on anyone separates you from that person and separates you from your Source because to judge or cast blame positions you in a lower based energy that places you at odds with another, and with your Source.

Do not allow the difference between danger and fear to confuse you. Danger is real, and if anyone poses a threat or danger then take the necessary precautions for their mind has been over run with fearful negativity. Fear, on the other hand, is not real. It is the anticipation of a negative outcome that may not even be present. Fear separates you from and blocks the potential of Love, true Love, human being to human being, self to self, for the Love that you withhold from another is the Love that you withhold from yourself.

Unconditional Love does not deny the ability to choose. Unconditional Love does not allow the helpless to suffer. Unconditional Love offers the basic right to all living organisms, which is to live.

Unconditionally, know what this means. Unconditionally, you are accepted. Unconditionally, you are approved. Unconditionally, you are loved no matter what your decision. Unconditionally, you are blessed whether you believe it to be true or not. With that being said, to find or carry any reason to withhold Unconditional Love from a brother or sister in the physical life experience is your personal choice to cast shadow on the Love that is offered to you by your Source.

Key:

Look inside for those things that separate you from others. What stops you from Loving Unconditionally? These ideas not only separate you from other human beings but they separate you from your Source, and you willingly place yourself in a negative, separatist vibration. Life is too short to subject yourself to that type of punishment. Choose differently. Choose Love for all and yourself.

Cycles & Seasons – Different Forms But The Same

The forms taken by the results you receive for your efforts are a direct reflection and presenting of the season for which you are prepared.

Mindset and awareness have a great deal to do with the season that you experience in the world. If you are only aware of the negative life situations and circumstances, then it is the only season that will take root and present itself in your life. As your effort moves you to grow in specific areas of your life, your understanding grows. What you believe is possible grows. What you see as possible grows. What you believe you are worthy of grows. You begin to see your goals within reach. You begin to look at those who have come before you, and succeeded where you have failed, as just regular men or women. This is what an increase in awareness does, and subtly your season in life changes.

A change in season can be a move from broken relationships to successful ones. It can be a move from not enough money to overflow and abundance. It can be a move from consistent ill health to health. There are various seasons that one can experience in life, but they are the result of the particular level of awareness in which you see life.

Most have a very narrow perspective of life. Most see only a narrow range of experiences, often their own particular experiences and ignore or set aside the lives being lived around them, especially if that life represents higher forms of living. That higher form of living, if noticed, is a source of pain and dissatisfaction to them. So, they attempt to tear it down in their minds with negative reasons for its purpose rather than seeing another's success as proof of the existence of possibility and opportunity.

The cycles that occur within the whole of society are an even greater, more wondrous task to fathom, but they exist. If one grasps the cycles of the world at this level they can influence culture and more. Music follows this trend. Clothing follows this trend. All of the arts and business efforts follow cyclical trends.

Just as nature has its seasons, all of life and the various, particular experiences have their seasons as well.

You must become a Master at recognizing the seasons in your life. You must become a Master at observing the crops you reap so that if a change in the seed sown the previous season is needed, you will be aware of the need. You, my friend, must be aware of the vast possibility and opportunities that exist as evidenced through the lives of countless others, and begin to tap into that greater awareness for your betterment.

Key:

Notice the patterns, the recurring themes in your life. Notice the changes that occur when you attempt to sow a different experience in the lives of those around you. Notice how you control the seasons in your life by holding fast to the knowing that what you want to experience exist as evidenced through others. Notice that every generation or so a new type of device or technology, that has enormous appeal or is of benefit to a wide range of society, appears. It is the result of seasons and cycles.

Community & Collaboration Is Easier Than You Think – Sharing Of Resources

When a group of human beings comes together as a means of support and protection, they make the decision to share. They share knowledge. They share physical resources and man hours. They share food. There is a high concern for each other's well-being. The entire group forms an extended family. There are elders, those with a wide range of knowledge, experience, and understanding. However, the disparity in age, knowledge or experience does not create ranks that would elevate one above another.

This worked in the smallest of tribes, and the same plan, the same philosophy can work on a global scale.

To start off, though, you can practice it in your home. Your children are not your children. You have been dawned with the responsibility of coaching and developing a brother or sister spiritual being for life in the physical realm. You do not lord over them; they do not owe you anything. It is merely your responsibility to model and create a foundation within them that will allow them to lead a life filled with ever increasing growth, experience, and expansion.

In the community of your home educate your clan of the maximum benefit to the sharing of resources, the sharing of duties in the local community, sharing in the awareness of the protection, safety, and uplift of the whole. Teach them to be independent, strong, and courageous in finding and following their path of service, which fully displays their gifts in the world. Teach them to collaborate with those who excel in skills that are not within their range of expertise.

If you teach these skills in the home, in your local community, then they will become the norm rather than the exception. It will become a greater, expanded way of life.

As it stands, resources are provided for all, and the accompanying ideas to harness those resources in the most effective and efficient way are plentiful. If energy is neither created nor destroyed, and merely changes form, then it stands to reason that energy can be harnessed and reused no matter what form it takes. But this has been missed or ignored by many. However, it can be yours; you can get it and use it.

Community and collaboration are simple staples of the mind. It is absolutely possible from nation to nation, from people to people. In today's age language should not be an issue, the blessing of skin tone should not be an issue, and personal preferences should not be an issue when it comes to sharing resources for the sustaining and advancing of the whole, not to mention the basic right to live.

Key:

Grow the sense of community within yourself and carry it everywhere you go. Know that your neighbor possesses powerful resources which could be of great benefit to the whole. Know that the development of those within your home is your responsibility. However the way you go about their training can condemn them to a life of misery or propel them to greatness. Look at the results obtained by others with the same teaching philosophy and the inner mental and outer physical experiences that surround them. Make the issue of community a way of life in your culture. Community and a deep Love for yourself and others solve more of the challenges of your world than you can imagine. Light begins to shine all around.

In Spirit I Thrive, In Mind I Fall. It Is My Job, To Unify Them All.

I now realize that for two decades I have been striving to release the true, authentic me that had been covered by fear-based ideas and perceptions. (Get Past Yourself)

I am realizing that the life I once lived, and the life story that is being lived around me by family and friends is not a chosen life, but one that has been passed along. With elements of fear at its base, loss, pain, failure, and the embarrassment of mistake once defined me, now they propel me. (The Other Side Of Fear)

Now I strive to allow the true, authentic, Source inspired me to breathe through at every moment. This grants me the knowing that my desires are pure and in line with the path that is specifically for me. (Allowing Me)

I did not need a teacher, a preacher, or a guru. All I needed was some Guidance and some Direction. (My Only Need)

Benny

The Rest Of The Series

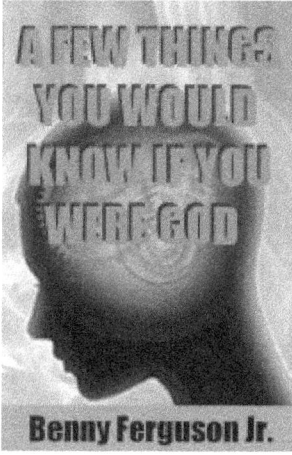

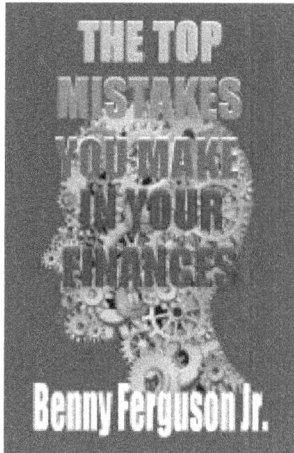

Connecting With Benny:

Facebook: www.facebook.com/bennyrfergusonjr

Youtube: www.youtube.com/BennyFergusonJr/videos

Twitter: www.twitter.com/BennyRFergusonJ

Contacting Benny:

Initial contacts to Benny for discussions, interviews, one – on - one or group coaching, speaking or training may be made through telephone or email.

Phone: 336-546-7142

Email: BennyFerguson@TheFergusonCompany.com